Doug Brainard

Threw These Eyes

Advice for Dads and Coaches

Threw
These Eyes

ADVICE FOR DADS AND COACHES

By Doug Brainard

Kravitz & Sons

INNOVATORS IN PUBLISHING, MARKETING AND ADVERTISING

Kravitz and Sons LLC
204 E Arlington Blvd. Suite B
Greenville, NC 27858

Published by Kravitz and Sons LLC.

ISBN: 979-8-89639-637-6 (sc)
ISBN: 979-8-89639-636-9 (e)

Table of Contents

DEDICATION

This book is dedicated to anyone who has donated time and effort to enrich the lives of the kids. This is not the Holy Grail of coaching; it's merely my perspective. No two people look at the same situation and see things in exactly the same way. I'm not the smartest guy in the world, ask anyone who knows me. Hopefully, this will help somebody.

Time is such a precious commodity; God bless all the people over the years, and the ones who will help in the years to come. You have no idea how much this means to some of these kids. Sometimes it's the only stability they have in their lives. Sometimes you can reach a child and help them change, or turn them in the right direction.

Growing up, I had nothing. Nobody wanted my brothers or me. Playing sports was the only refuge I had. Once on the field or on the court, I could free my mind, soul, and body and play a game, and I did not worry about my pathetic life. Many times, in my early years, I would dream of how cool it would be if the coach were my dad. In my thirty-three years of coaching, the kids have said they wished I were their dads. It melts my heart. I've always felt if I could make a child feel good about himself, or ease her burden in any way, even if for fleeting moments, my job at the park is complete. Make a difference in your town.

Thanks to all the coaches that helped me in my early years. I couldn't have made it without you! That's why I always try to return the favor, over and over. Thanks.

I would like to acknowledge the help of Betty-Ruth, who corrected all my mistakes, Mike for printing it out, and my kids helping every step of the way. Special thanks go out to The Big-Show, John-Boy, and Billy, for giving me the idea, from one of their playhouses. You people made it all possible.

PREP

If you're lucky enough to play at a new park, you're definitely in the minority. Most Little League parks are old and worn. With this being said, all the parks need work before the season begins. Everyone needs to get out and help. There are many problems and items that need to be fixed, cleaned, or painted. I also realize that most people are in the work force, but the time you contribute to the ball fields yields a great benefit to your child and to other children.

You don't have to be a professional in any trade to help out, but professionals are always greatly welcomed. Helping in any form or fashion, at any time, is always appreciated. Plumbing is always a major problem in restrooms – there's no telling what has been dumped in them over the years.

Like life, things always go in cycles. Kids are always moving up in leagues in two- or three-year cycles. Some have brothers and sisters going through the league at different times. Whenever this happens, the park becomes the kids' and parents' second home. These are usually the people that end up donating their time and efforts to the park.

The casual observer has no idea how many countless hours have been invested long before the first pitch. Meetings start taking place months before the season gets underway. It takes a lot to get the league up and running, creating the league budget, planning game and practice schedules, and raising money any way possible for equipment and uniforms. It takes lots of money to run a league for a summer. Hopefully your league will have some extra money, but this is rare. So, if you are not able to donate your time, cash donations are always welcomed.

Any park in the country cannot be run without help from of women. In most leagues, men hold down the presidency or vice presidency, but the real work comes from being the secretary, treasurer, or the head of the concession stand. All the money made in the stand goes to paying the umpires. Help in the concession stands is voluntary, but it seems to be the same people helping all the time!

Little League is all non-profit, and it relies on people donating their time. Everyone wants to watch their children play, therefore help out before or after games. The ladies that help run the concession stand do the same repetitive, thankless jobs that no one sees.

Just like at the house, this reminds me of a lot of husbands. They have no idea what it takes to run a household. Lots of guys don't know or care about how everything gets accomplished. But it always does and usually by the same people whether it's at the house or the park. Kudos to all you mothers that work three jobs: home, work, and the park. I don't know how you do it. More moms should be coaching; they know just as much as the guys. There are just too many other things that are taken for granted. Make yourself more aware and be more contentious with others. Help in any way possible, and all you dads out there, buy your wives some jewelry and take them out to eat. Help out at the house and at the park.

I can't say this enough: Kids should get their gear ready the night before a practice or a game. Parents have a busy schedule. It's tough enough with one child, but when you have a number of children, it's crazy. Preparing their gear the night before prevents them from missing any items once they get to the park. This also helps the kids arrive at the park on time. Children need some responsibility at an early age. Getting their things ready is not that big of a job, but it really helps out.

Getting to the park on time is a big problem for some. Help prevent the coach from having a panic attack because the kids aren't on time for the game. Coaches have to turn in their lineups fifteen minutes before the game. Some players are always late. I know we live in a busy world, but please make an effort to arrive on time. Coaches, when the players finally arrive, do not badger them about being late. They are not the ones doing the driving, so just relax and control your emotions.

People, whether we are at the park or at the house, we need to do a better job recycling our trash. I know at the park we're playing a game, but I'm talking about the game of life. Believe me, we will be dead and gone before there's a big problem, but our children and their children will have to deal with it. This is a correctable error, but we need to address this now! We are running out of room for landfills! Please, let's make a better effort to recycle, at home, at work, and at the park. Remember, it's for our children.

We need to get the whole community involved in our parks. In other cultures, older people are coveted and held in the highest esteem. In our world, we put them out to pasture and no one has time for them. We need to get them out and about. Kids need to be around senior citizens. Nothing lights up older people more than being around kids. Older people have already experienced life many times over. Kids can learn a lot from them. All too often, no one has time to listen to the elderly or to show them any attention. Most of the time, the only people they have to talk to are telemarketers and TV preachers, and both groups want their money. We come into this world as babies and our parents help to nurture and to love us as we grow. As the years progress, our parents may eventually revert back into children, needing help with the simplest of life's demands! If in fact they lose their driver's license, their independence is gone. They become prisoners within their own homes. So, let's all remember who took care of us when we were young. Get senior citizens involved in our school system and get them to the ballparks. Baseball was the sport in their day.

DADS/COACHES

All parents want the best for their kids, so when you throw your hat into the coaching ring, certain things must be observed. Coaches' sons or daughters always seem to get the raw end of the deal. Sometimes we expect too much from our kids. Dads have a way of being harder on their own kids, while being easier on the other players. You have to be a special person to be able to keep this balance. I wish I could have been one of those people.

We cannot live through our children. They have to live their own lives; therefore, don't try to play through their eyes. Dads have to walk a fine line when coaching. Sometimes dads have to watch how hard they push. There's a big difference between coaching and drilling and too often this line gets crossed.

It's every dad's dream to have his child play a game professionally or to get a college scholarship. This rarely happens, so relax! Always coach in a manner that is easily digestible for the kids. Have fun, excite their minds, and always praise them for working hard and hustling. I seem to not do this enough. Dads, watch the drilling and pushing too hard. It's tough on your kids and your spouse, whether at the park or at house. Keep the peace! Dads will also go over what happened or what didn't happen after the game on the ride home, belaboring the point. Relax! Like I say, learn from my mistakes; old dogs can learn new tricks.

Coach with compassion and patience. Kids absorb things so quickly, so all we have to do is motivate with the right perspective. Teams are allowed three coaches—two on the field coaching the bases, plus one in the dugout. I cannot emphasize how important the dugout coach is to the team. Not only does that coach have to watch the kids, they have to be able to keep up with the batting line-up, have the players pay attention to the game, and tell them what went on (and what should have gone on) during the game. Lots of coaching needs to be done from the bench. Pick your coaches wisely, always keeping in perspective that it's a ball game!

When coaching, always remember back when we were kids. Things that were new and different were pretty scary. Repetition and practice will cure these feelings. Remember, try as we might; kids have to cut their own trail, live it, and learn it. They have to make their own choices through gentle suggestions from Mom and Dad. With some kids, you need to take a different approach. Try to get them to do what you want, without them knowing that you want them to do it. Through diligence and practice, things will come easier for the players.

After the kids reach thirteen years of age, Little League is over. At this age you have to earn your way on a team. This is usually when most kids quit playing baseball, so treasure the time you have while they're young. After Little League, it seems their innocence is gone. People are creatures of habit, so have fun and be creative in your coaching, and don't act like a fool in front of the crowd and your team during the game. The way the team acts and plays is a direct reflection of the coach, therefore, be calm and relax! Like I say, "It's what the kids want out of it, not what you want."

Have compassion and patience. Live and learn something every day, then apply the thing we learned. Coaches, some kids are disruptive, and time-consuming. They goof off or just want your constant attention. Remember they probably don't get much attention at home. Try not to be so tough on these kids. Years ago, my wife worked at daycare centers. When I come to pick up our kids, I would play with the other children at the center. Most of the children would play nicely, but I could always tell the kids that didn't have a dad or the kids that didn't get any attention at the house. They would be mean as heck, pinching, kicking, or hitting. They were this way to get attention from their peers. Watch out for this and be gentle with them. Sometimes any attention is better than nothing. With some children, you have no idea what they have to go through just to make it to practice or to the game.

Everybody wants to be needed, everybody needs to be wanted, and everybody needs to be loved. Coaches, keep your eye out for these kids. They need to have love, attention, and patience thrown in their direction. Like a lot of things we take for granted, things that seem small and insignificant to some affect others in a very profound way. So, like they say, "Walk a mile in my shoes." Again, coach with patience and compassion.

HITTING

Hitting the ball on any level of play is the best part of the game. Playing the field is a lot different than hitting in that, when we're playing the field and surrounded by players, it's easier to take if we drop or miss a ball or make a mistake. Once kids get to the plate, however, they are alone on an island! At the plate, they're in front of friends, family, and peers. This is where pressure, stress, hopes, and dreams all occur.

Parents, this is where all the practice in the backyard comes into play. In the early years, it is imperative to hit the ball. Once you get the kids comfortable hitting the ball, everything else will fall into place. If your kids play long enough, you'll see that each coach has his own theory on hitting. By the time the kids enter high school, their swings will have been broken down many times. If they can hit the ball, I don't mess with their swing. Everyone has their own swing; you just have to find it.

Simply put, hitting is timing and being comfortable. Sports, like life, offers many learning experiences. Being comfortable makes everything easier, especially in the early years. The things we teach now, if taught properly, lay the groundwork for a foundation. Each time we play or practice, make sure something is learned from it. Every time we play or practice, it's a learning block. The idea here is to get the kids to react, not think, just to flow with the game.

Some kids have awkward swings, but if they're hitting the ball leave them alone. I had to learn this the hard way. My son would hammer the ball to right field. One of the guys I coached with asked why my boy never hit the ball to left field. Well, I started working with him trying to get him to pull the ball. After working extensively on this, he got to where he couldn't hit the ball with a tennis racket. He got frustrated. After one hitting session, he commented that he always hit the ball until I started working with him on pulling the ball. Believe me, this ripped my heart out! It liked to have killed me. Finally, after lots of practice and patience, he got back on track. As Yogi says, "If it ain't broke, don't fix it!"

You can't hit what you can't see. Keep your head on the ball. Conventional wisdom is to have your feet shoulder-width apart, knees slightly bent. Make sure your elbows are away from your body. Keep the hands up. Make sure the bat is at the proper angle so that you can get the bat though the strike zone easily and quickly. Some people teach stepping, some don't. If you're going to step, make sure you're stepping toward the pitcher, keeping your momentum going in that direction. Some teach pivoting on the back foot, squashing the bug. Make sure when you start your swing that the bat head goes toward the plate, not your batting helmet. It's all bat speed that makes the ball jump off the bat. When you swing the bat you should hear the bat cutting through the wind, making a bumblebee sound! Whoa! Throw your hands through the zone. Following through is important.

When holding the bat, you don't have to squeeze the life out of it. Have a good hold on it, but don't squeeze it. Attack the ball! Know the strike zone and hit strikes! Coaches want the kids to swing the bat, but the kids have to develop an eye for the strike zone. Kids, you can't make a living hitting pitcher pitches. Simply put, it's hard to hit balls out of the strike zone. Some kids are bad-ball hitters. In the long run, you have to swing at strikes. Take what the other team gives you. All we are looking to do is get on base and roll the lineup over. Batters, with two strikes, choke up on the bat and make contact—put the ball in play! Make the defense make a play. Protect the plate with two strikes; go down swinging on anything close! Don't hold the bat on strike three; this drives the coach crazy! Pull the trigger. Don't let the ump have the last say in the matter. Once you hit it, run and don't look at the ball.

One of the biggest problems for the kids when moving up in the leagues from coach-pitch to live pitching is the unknown factor of where the ball is going. Kids get comfortable having the ball cross the plate regularly, whether it's from an adult pitching or from the pitching machine. But put a kid on the mound and they worry about getting hit! Once they start thinking about this, they step out of the batter's box before the pitcher even delivers the ball to the plate. When this happens, they shorten the bat; therefore, they have less plate coverage, and when the feet go, the hips and the head will follow. If they hit the ball, it's only with their arms, or it's fouled off. When we are playing any sport, we try to incorporate the whole body. Use it all. Throwing or hitting, we have to get our legs into the equation. The lower part of your body is the strongest!

The transition period between the pitching machine and coach-pitching to live pitching is enormous. When the kids are playing with the machine, the ball is across the plate every time (unless the ball is wet). The kids get into a comfort zone swinging the bat the way you want them to, but when it comes to live pitching, nobody knows where the ball is going. Kids also get into a comfort zone when Dad pitches to them all the time. They know Dad won't hit them. That's why it's good to get their brothers, sisters, uncles, or friends pitching to them. They have to see different pitchers with different arm angles. Stepping out can easily be remedied by laying a bat about a foot behind the batter's legs, parallel to the plate. If they step out when they swing, they land on the bat. They are so conscious about the bat being behind them that their swings are going to be awkward for several swings, but they will get the hang of it. Like anything, through practice and repetition they will master it. If you're going to step, stride toward the pitcher keep your momentum moving in the direction where the ball is going.

Coaches, make sure the young kids have batting helmets that fit tight. It's hard to hit the ball if you swing and the helmet moves, blocking your vision. Hitting is one of the best things about baseball, so make sure it's a joy for the kids, and not a burden.

FIELDING

First and foremost, you have to pay attention when you're fielding. Watch the ball and the batter. Most baseball injuries occur when the ball hits players who are not paying attention and those injuries can be serious. You have to be ready to field the ball, or at least deflect it—protect yourself, and use the glove. Early in the baseball lives of our kids, I started out using a tennis ball. This does two things. First, the biggest problem catching the ball at this age is getting hit with the ball. Believe me, if they get hit, it will leave a lasting impression on them. Some players will get so scared that they won't play anymore. Playing catch with a tennis ball won't hurt even if it hits them. Start out catching without a glove until they master it. Secondly, when catching a tennis ball with their glove, the ball will squirt out because it is very light.

Learning to catch a tennis ball with a glove will teach the players to use two hands. This will help you hold the ball in your glove, plus your hand is on the ball, ready to throw. These techniques, learned early, will turn into double plays later on in your baseball life. When watching TV, lay on your back and toss a tennis ball to the ceiling, and catch it with your glove hand. This will teach you to cushion the ball as it drops in your hand. Slightly pull your hands back as the ball comes to you, this will take the sting out of the ball. Use soft hands.

When fielding the ball, conventional wisdom is to have one foot slightly in front of the other, knees slightly bent, and rear end down. You have to be able to go left and right, forward and backward. Get the glove low. It's easier to bring the glove up than down. Stay in front of the ball. This way if the ball takes a bad hop, you can deflect it off your body. Use your glove and your body to swipe through the ball. On short hops, if you don't catch it, knock the ball down in front of you. Practicing with a tennis ball on short hops will teach you to get in front of the ball and bring your glove through the ball without getting hurt.

Always come to the ball, play it on your hop. This cuts the batter's lead down on running to the base and puts your feet in position to throw the ball. Whenever the ball gets behind you, turn to your glove-side to throw. This is a natural motion, instead of turning the wrong way and having to turn in a circle to get your feet in position. Proper turning helps you get rid of the ball quicker, getting the ball back into play. Turning the wrong way or holding the ball for only a few seconds with a player running at full speed can mean up to ten feet on the base paths, and that's a lot. This also keeps the double play in order and keeps the runner from getting into scoring position. When playing the outfield, never drift to the ball on a popup or fly ball. Run hard to the spot and adjust to it. I always like my players to toss up some grass to test the wind so they know which direction the wind's blowing.

To play defense requires paying attention, knowing the situation, and knowing where you're going with the ball when it comes to you. Players always need to know how many outs there are. We're all going to make mistakes, so know where you're going with the ball should it get by you. Don't compound mistakes. Say you drop a ball or it gets by you; make sure you still throw it to the right bag. You have to know how many outs there are and where the base runners are positioned. Playing defense sometimes will put you in a coma. Whether it's from walks, errors, or hits, every play should have the fielders moving and backing up people. Always shout encouraging words to your pitcher. Players, remember to do some house cleaning in your area. Simply put, pick up the rocks! When fielding, you can't do anything until you catch the ball. Move your feet and look the ball into your glove and squeeze it. Be calm, and that calm comes from inner confidence in your ability. Say, I've already been there and done that, through repetition and practice. Just relax and do it.

Throwing, like hitting, is off the back leg. Most of the power is in your lower body. You have to get the entire body into motion. Use it all! You have to get your feet in the proper position. Get the ball out of your glove, and throw it—nobody can outrun the ball. Arm extension is very important. You have to spread your wings wide, bend your back, and follow through. Any sport you play, follow-through is important. Most sports involve the same movements with slight variations. When fielding the ball, open your hands wide. Lots of kids use brand-new gloves, so make sure the gloves are oiled up so they can open and close well. Make sure you open up your hand and glove so you're catching the ball with more surface area.

Just like most sports, ball-handling skills are important. Transferring all is critical in turning double plays. Use two hands on the ball. This helps you hold it in your glove, plus your hand is on the ball, ready to throw. This is always the difference between the runner beating the throw by a step or being thrown out by a step. A good drill for this, once again, is to use a tennis ball with two people playing catch with two balls. Good hand-and-eye coordination is needed. Practice, practice, practice, will turn into the pitcher's best friend—the double play. When fielding the ball, always use the glove. Some kids like to field balls hit slowly to them bare-handed, but all too many times they look up or forget the ball. Players, wait until your hands get bigger to try to one-hand the ball.

Defense, in pickles or run downs, the object is to get the out, or make the runner go back to their base. But to do this, we have to limit our throws. The more you throw the ball around, the more chances you take on throwing it away. Always give yourself a good angle to throw—especially catchers; take a step toward the pitcher when throwing the ball to third. Make fewer than two throws and get the out.

Fielders in run downs, have the ball in your throwing hand. Pump the ball at the player while you're running at them. Always give the person receiving the ball time to catch the ball and apply the tag. You can't get on top of the person your throwing to, therefore, don't get too close to them and fire the ball. Give them time! When applying the tag, use two hands on the ball. Sometimes when runners slide, they will knock the ball out of your glove.

Pitchers, on come-backers with a runner on second and nobody else on base, catch the ball, turn and freeze the runner, and run right at them. If they go back to the bag, go to first with it. Make sure you chase them back to the bag.

When playing the infield, you have to watch for aggressive players rounding the bag too far, and be ready to throw behind them for the out. Before batters reach the box, size them up. Usually the bigger players are the slowest. Know how much time you have to make a play or make an educated guess. You have to be in a hurry when making plays, but don't rush it! Focus on good foot work and making solid throws. Relax and trust your ability, stay within yourself. Don't try and do too much, or the impossible! Sometimes the best throws are the ones we don't throw. Hold the ball, if the player already has first base. A wild throw puts the runner on second or third base. Keep them from getting in scoring position and keep the double play in order. Help yourself and the pitcher. We always want to get the lead runner on plays, but if the ball is hit at a bag, take the out. Late in the game, situations may change, but until then, get the out!

Players, know the base runners. Watch how they run though the bag and watch how they get off the base on a foul ball. Aggressive players will tell on themselves by the way they play the game. They play aggressively in every phase of the game: fielding, hitting, and running. If they get on, they are going to try and take an easy base. Take advantage of this, if you can. Players of this nature are going to try to steal second base. The catcher and the shortstop had better be paying attention when the runner plans to take off. It's nice if you can throw them out, but a lot of the time, they make it in safe.

With no one on first, the rule of thumb on second base states, "With less than two outs, never run on a ball hit in front of you." Run only on a ball hit behind you. Shortstops and the people playing third base can easily throw out the aggressive player on a ball hit to either of them. Like always, you can't do anything until you catch the ball. Come get it, play it on your hop, and keep your feet in position. Don't even look at the runner, but give a hard fake to first base as if you're throwing the ball. You have to make good fakes to the runners to have them buy into the decoys. As sure as the nose on my face, the aggressive runner will be moving in your direction, thinking they have third base easily. This leads to an easy tag-out or throw-out. When trying this play, make sure you give yourself plenty of time to throw to first if the runner isn't coming.

Second basemen, if there's a runner on second, only throw to third if you glove the ball cleanly! Otherwise go to the closest bag for the out. Remember when playing second base, you have all the time in the world to get the out at first. You can drop the ball, kick it, and fall on it, and as long as you stay with it, you'll still make the play.

First basemen should know their range as well the range of your teammate playing second. A good first baseman will stretch to the ball on a throw to first, but always see where the throw is going to come from. Sometimes it might be in the front or the backside of the bag. So don't stretch too soon, it's hard to maneuver if you're stretched out of position. When playing first with nobody on base, and the batter hits a double, back up second on a throw from the outfield, especially from left field. When stretching to make the catch, if the throw goes wide, come off the base to make the play. We can't have a throw get away, which moves the runner into scoring position. Come off the bag and smother the ball—keep it in front of you. Poor throws from the shortstop usually hit directly behind the first baseman. These throws don't get too far because they're in a straight line. Throws that get away usually come from third or plays in front of the plate. These throws are coming from angles, and the balls hit the fence and bounce away. That's why right fielders have to be moving to back up the play.

Balls hit by a lefthander to left field will tail away from outfielders to the right side, and balls hit by a right hander to right field will tail to the left. Outfielders, when you're not involved in a play, move and back up a bag. Stay active! Don't go to sleep. Talk it up. Move! First things first; you can't do anything, until you catch the ball!

PRACTICE

Coaches, it's hard to practice when it's cold. You can't get too much accomplished. All the kids are thinking about is how to stay warm.

It always seems that the first couple of practices are cold and rainy. About all you can get done is some conditioning and stretching drills. Parents, make sure your children wear the proper clothing for the first few practices. I don't know how many times I have seen kids come to the park wearing just a tee shirt. The parents will be bundled up with coats and blankets, or they'll just drop their children off and leave because it's too cold to watch.

Come on parents, common sense and logic will carry a person a long way in life. Use your heads! Get some clothes on your children. Coaches address this at the first practice with the parents. The coaches' job is to coach. We are not their moms or dads, and we're not here to discipline your kids. This needs to be done at home. I don't know how many times I've heard this over the years. Parents, you know your children, so help the coaches out with your child's attitudes. Coaching at times turns into cheap babysitting.

Any good coach starts out the season by telling the players what is expected of them; nothing out of the ordinary. The coach is looking for three things: to listen, to try, and to hustle. The rest is gravy. Once something bad happens, you can't change it, so just play through it. During games or practices, I never let the kids use words such as dumb, stupid, or shut up. If young kids hear dumb or stupid too many times, they will start believing it. Anybody who talks like that on my field has to run laps.

To play any sport or to be any kind of an athlete or player, you cannot dwell on mistakes. Somewhere down the road, you'll get another chance, so you've got to be ready. Don't worry about spilt milk. What's done is done; play on.

Most practices only last for ninety minutes. This is not much time to run a practice. It is very important when the kids are young to get in the backyard with your children, even if it's just fifteen minutes a day. This benefits them and yourself. It's like sending your children to school to learn—the teacher can't do it all. You just can't turn your children over to them and expect them to teach everything. We have to help out starting at home. I love to get players' parents practicing with them. When I practice, I get moms and dads on the field, playing the game. It's good for the kids to see the coach or their parents mess up or make a mistake, so they know it's going to happen and it's all right. No one is perfect. Parents, when playing catch in the backyard, be sure you have a wall or a fence behind you. That way, if you miss the ball or a bad throw, you don't have to walk far to get the ball. Parents, just like the kids, you need to stretch before you start.

To practice soft-toss in the back yard, throw a blanket over a clothesline. Then, get a bucket to sit on and let the kids hit the ball into the blanket. Using Wiffle or golf balls works great too, and you don't have to chase the balls too far. This helps them develop great hand and eye coordination, even if you only practice for fifteen minutes a day. You and your child will benefit from this exercise. I find that when I come home from work and I'm worn out, exercising or playing with the kids seems to rejuvenate me.

Get in the backyard and practice with the kids; they love this. Get off the couch and get involved! Do your coaching in the backyard. Don't wait till you get to the game, standing behind the backstop barking instructions to your children.

Coaches, you're only given an hour and half, so you'd better be pretty organized. This can be another one of my faults, but I always surround myself with good people who have the skills I lack. My forte is dealing with the players. Make sure you have your pitching, hitting, and fielding going on at the same time. Try to keep everybody busy. Practicing for an hour and a half doesn't give much time to get things done, so have your practices broken down into time frames. You have to be able to address all issues and situations pertaining to the game.

Coaches, when dealing with young players, hugs will go a long way toward making them feel wanted and comfortable. This will in turn help with your teaching. I didn't get many hugs when I was young, but I make up for it now when I'm coaching. Incorporate this in your coaching. When playing in games, when it comes down to the last outs, whether you're on offense or defense, if something bad happens on the last out, the players will carry this to the next game. We as coaches have to make sure that our players understand that we play a long game. The plays we make and the ones we don't add up to the total sum of the game. The runners we leave on base when we're batting, or the runners we let score when we're fielding, also help determine the outcome of the game—it's never the last out. Make sure this is clearly understood to all players and parents. When bad things happen, a hotdog and a coke will go a long way in washing the blues away after the game. I don't agree with a lot of things that Bobby Knight has to say, but he always talks about the five P's—"Proper Planning Prevents Poor Performance"—and he's right. We have to cross all the bridges before we come to them in practice, and cover all the bases. Go over every possible scenario or situation that could possibly happen in a game. Make sure the kids can understand and digest the information you're trying to convey to them in the simplest and most creative way. I compare this to a few teachers who teach the same boring text day after day. We have to excite the mind! (In no way am I trying to slam teachers. Everyone knows they have a tough, low paying job. Imagine that, the people molding our children's minds getting paid next to nothing—go figure.) Just make sure the children have a firm grasp on what you're teaching in practice. Kids are more likely to listen, remember, and understand information that is presented creatively. The players have to trust and believe in you, and what you say.

Practice running the bases. Once you've earned your way on base, via a walk or hit, be smart! When the ball is hit directly to the second basemen and you are on first, you cannot run into the tag—this turns into an easy double play. You can't run out of the baseline or you're out. If they field it cleanly, stop and make them go to second for the out.

When you're on second with nobody on first, if the ball is hit to the shortstop or third, make them look at you by busting off the bag hard for a couple of steps. This helps the batter running down the line, and gives them a little more time to make it to first. You have to get the fielders' attention. After they throw the ball to first, hustle to third. Make sure they throw the ball—a good shortstop or third baseman will fake a throw, then throw behind you. Don't let them fake you out of your socks. It doesn't make a difference if you're playing offense or defense, make good fakes, sell them! With less than two outs, make sure you go half-way on pop-ups. Listen to your coaches.

Never slide into first base unless you're trying to avoid a tag. This only happens when the first basemen is pulled up the line on a bad throw. Not sliding properly can result in a lot of strawberries or brush burns on your legs. To practice the art of sliding, get a big piece of cardboard and start on a slight grade (the way you do when learning to ride a bike). Slide with one leg extended and the other leg bent, with your ankle under the back of your knee. Make sure you land on your rump. Practice on the cardboard until you master this technique. The ground can be very unforgiving. Don't roll to the side. This is how strawberries occur. Just like anything, we learn through repetition.

Dads, when pitching batting practice to young kids, throw tennis balls to them. Throw some pitches for strikes, and throw some at them. They have to practice getting out of the way of the ball. Most players will turn and leave their backs exposed. The back is a big target. We have to teach them how to turn and roll away from the pitch. The idea here is to take a glancing blow, if any. Young players have a big fear of getting hit by the pitch. Tackle this phobia early and often. They can't act like deer in headlights! Another way of getting the players comfortable at the plate is to have the coach pitch to them without the players swinging the bat. Have them watch the ball all the way to the catcher's glove. While doing this, have the batter call out if it was a ball or a strike. Remember, hitting is timing and being comfortable.

Coaches and parents, when at the park practicing with the team, don't make all the plays when the kids hit the ball. Let the ball drop in or make it look close, but let it fall. On ground balls, scoop them up, slide step, and make them run hard through the bag. Make good throws, but let them beat it out. It's no fun for them if you make all the plays.

Coaches, don't let your pitchers fall in love with the curve ball at a young age. This can hurt their arm. All they need is a change-up to get the batter off-balance. Too many players hurt their arms trying to throw curves. Wait until their arms have developed.

All smart coaches have a calling tree for practices and games. I love working with the players, but I don't like calling people. Make your life easier; this is the only way to go.

In all my years of coaching, one thing has stayed the same. At the end of every game or practice, mothers seem to always carry the players' bags. What's up with this? Your mother has been taking care of you since birth. Kids, at least carry your own bag. Come on, get with it! Help out. Coaches, not too many people I know love to go to work, but you can't make practice like a job for the players. That way you will never get anything accomplished. Keep it fun and informative.

THE GAME

Never call the coach about possible rainouts. Coaches can call off practices, but games are a different story. It's one thing if it has been raining all day. Our league runs like lots of tournaments—show up and see, unless there comes a toad-strangler. Game-time decisions are made by a committee at the park. The coach doesn't know if the team is playing, and it's not the coaches' decision. You have to show up to the park to see if you're playing. Coaches, make sure you go over this in the first practice, but doing so rarely helps. Parents will have their children call the house, so I can't chew them out, but once the parents get to the park, I give them an earful!

Parents, do not show up to practice or to the game with food! Nothing is more disruptive than food. Most of the players are watching that one child eat, let alone that player, having to go to the bathroom halfway through the game.

Coaches can't coach without players. Getting there early allows the players time to stretch properly and get their arms loose. This takes more than ten minutes, and is very important. Once you've got the team assembled, make sure everyone has their shoes tied and has been to the bathroom before they hit the field. When entering the field after a game, make sure your team stays out of the way, so the team leaving the dugout has time to clean up and leave. This is always a problem; therefore, stay back. When the team gets to the dugout, it's time for the parents to sit in the stands and leave the coaching for the coach.

Get little Tommy or Jody a Gatorade before the game starts, not during the game! Make sure the players hang their bat bags up, or put them out of the way, so nobody trips or falls on them. Coaches, put your lineup where the kids can see it, but can't touch it. Magnetic boards never work. The players lose the magnets after the second game. During the pre-game warm-ups, I make sure the other coaches hit infield and outfield to the kids, so I can walk the infield telling my players to relax and let the game come to them. I also pick up rocks that find their way to the infield. Believe me, it's no fun having a ball hit a rock, jump up and pop you in the chin, let alone sliding on one going into a base. Pick them up; the players will appreciate it.

Before the game, there always seems to be a parent who will bring gum for all the teammates. This is fine, as long as all the wrappers find their way to the trashcan. Please don't throw your gum on the field when you're done with it.

In the early years of the player's baseball lives, some coaches like to have the kids chattering, when playing defense. I personally don't believe in this, but if you're going to let your team talk it up, make sure they're not hollering, "Batter can't hit or swing!" It's tough enough at this early age without the added pressure.

Players, never take your glove to the plate with you, and never take your bat to the outfield. This means if you strike out, and you will, don't worry about it when you go to the outfield on defense. Or if you miss a ball while playing defense, don't worry about it at the plate. Once you get to the Little League level, umpires call the balls and strikes. It has been my experience to make sure the kids pull up their pants to their knees. This gives the umpires a good look at where the strike zone should end. This works great with contrasting colors on the pants and socks.

Try to help out the umps anytime you can. Umpires are human too, and they're going to make mistakes. All you're asking from an ump is to be consistent—good, bad, or indifferent. Not all umpires are petty, but there are a few. Coaches, don't cause uproars in the players or the people in the stands after a bad call. Be diplomatic; pull the ump off to the side to express your views. Don't rant and rave in front of the kids. Umpires never like being showed up in front of a crowd. Watch what you say. Before every game, I talk to the players about taking the parents and the umpires out of the game. Kids see the coach and hear the parents complaining about the calls, and the next thing you know, they're whining and not playing. Umpires are like everybody else; they have to work. If they are older gentlemen, their knees are killing them if they work the plate. Therefore, respect the umpires and their calls.

Kids, with two strikes, protect the plate! Choke up on the bat and put the ball in play, if the pitch is close! Don't let the umpire ring you up. Never hold the bat on a third strike. The coach will pull out his or her hair. I used to have a head full of hair before I started coaching.

Help yourself and the coach out; on anything close; take a rip. Coaches, help yourselves out by not belaboring a bad call by the ump. They're not going to change their calls! With some umpires, the only call they're going to change is every call after this one! Remember who is watching you. Kids will see all, and tell all. So relax, and lead by example.

The crowds at tee-ball, coach-pitch, or machine-pitch always seem to be the rowdiest. Grandma and Grandpa, Mom and Dad often scream so loud, you'd think you were at the World Series. Coaches and people in the stands need to let the scorekeeper do his job. People scream about the scoring right after a play happens. Relax; they will get it right! Coaches at tee-ball and training league games, don't run the players wild on the basepaths. It's one thing on solid hits, but on overthrows in the infield, hold your players on the base. Lots of coaches get caught up in the game, influenced by the cheering crowd when players are young. Don't send the runners, especially when you're beating the tar out of the other team. This does nothing good for the other team's psyche. The better team usually wins out, so don't pour salt in the wound.

Scoring players on solid hits is a horse of a different color. Have you ever seen any professional athlete close their eyes while on the on-deck circle, swinging a bat, or a fielder making a throw? Or someone on the free throw line shooting the shot, or runners standing in the starters blocks with their eyes closed? In any sport, this applies. Through positive thinking, and mental imagery, they're playing the action in their minds before it happens and seeing themselves being successful. Through positive thinking, and mental imagery. Just like anything, this takes practice and staying calm, and this inner calm comes from relaxing and relying on your confidence in your ability. Players think, I have already been there and done this many times over, through practice and games. Do what you know how to do, and don't try too much, or try too hard. If you try too hard, what ends up happening is that you will start pressing! Pressing occurs when you try and try so hard to do something and you start working against yourself. Relax and be calm. I always tell my players to take a deep breath and blow it out before any play. Once this is done, complete the play.

All the coaching needs to be done in practice. If the kids don't know it by game time, I've always thought, it's the coaches' fault. Game time is when the kids are on stage. They are in front of the world—friends, family, and peers. So, coaches, don't get on anyone during the game if something bad happens (and it will). During the game all I ever say is, "It's all right," and give the palms down sign, meaning be calm!

Parents, when you get to the park, the players are in the hands of the coaches. When they hit the field, leave them alone. They cannot receive instructions from everyone and the coach at the same time. Parents, do your coaching in the backyard! Use positive reinforcement only. No instructions. It's hard enough for the coaches to keep the players' attention without instructions coming from the bleachers. Let the coaches do their job. Coaches and parents, don't say, "No pressure" in pressure situations. We cannot plant seeds in their head. Let them play.

The game mirrors life—you have to be adaptable and flexible, and work together to get along. We have to learn how to win and lose. Life doesn't let us win all the time. I've always believed that losing builds humility, and humility builds character. Losing a ball game just means the other team was better prepared that day. Winning ball games will be a byproduct of listening, learning, and having fun in practice. I once had an old coach who told me, "Never let your highs get too high, or your lows too low."

ALL-STARS

We have devised a plan for naming all-stars in our league. Our president phones the parents the night after the closing ceremony to avoid embarrassment to any player or parents. Players and parents alike get disappointed during the ceremony if they are not selected. Some players get their hearts broken in front of a large crowd, and this is not good. Better to save everybody's feelings and call the next day.

There's always controversy at all-star time. People wonder how one player made it and another didn't. There's high anxiety for players and parents. Lots of parents complain that coaches' kids always make all-stars. The simple fact is that lots do because their parents, the coaches, work with them away from practice. They practice with them all the time. Anywhere in the country, you are going to have small-town politics. It's a fact of life, and you have to deal with it and play above it. You can't worry about things you can't control, because that taxes the mind and the body. Hearts will always get broken this time of the year. The players always know who should make the team. The coaches are the ones who select the players. So, if your child doesn't make the team, hopefully this will make them hungrier so they will practice harder and more diligently for next year.

Life's not fair. They say things that don't kill you only make you stronger. It's hard for kids to buy into this, but everything's a learning experience. Life's a long arduous trek, so live and learn always. Coaches, make sure the kids you have selected are going to be in town. Lots of people go on vacation at this time of the year, and if they do, you catch a bunch of flack from the parents of kids who didn't make the team. So save yourself the headaches, you already have enough.

Coaches, when you're out of town, make sure you clean up the dugouts after games. Win or lose, some teams think they get a raw deal during the game and leave the dugouts a mess. This again falls back to the volunteers of the park, and as I stated earlier, any help is appreciated. Plus, this doesn't look good on your team or your town. Do the right thing!

Parents, all-star time is when the pressure is really on the children, so make sure they act in a mannerly fashion at the game. One year my team played a team, where the crowd would scream "Swing," in unison as the ball crossed the plate. Let the kids play ball, and let them decide the outcome of the game. Offer positive reinforcement only, not all the other crap—remember they're only kids. Children are a product of their environment, so act right!

Parents, most tournaments are out of town, and usually an hour or so away. Therefore, when driving in a caravan to the parks, you don't have to stick your bumper up the next car's tailpipe! Give them some room; they're not going to run off and leave you! So many times over the years, I've seen parents driving so close to the car in front of them that you practically couldn't fit a piece of paper between the bumpers. Be careful and make it to the park in one piece. Be safe and sound!

Sometimes, all-star time for the older players marks the last games they will be playing, whether they move on to another sport or just give up the game totally. Make sure it's an enjoyable experience for them, because they will remember this for a lifetime. The ultimate goal at all-star time is to have a team make it to the Little League World Series in Pennsylvania, which is the dream of any Little League player or coach. Don't let petty jealousy and animosity rule your life. That's what's wrong with the world today. We have to get along with everyone. Grow up and put your differences aside. We have to be part of the solution, not the problem. We have to learn something every day, and apply the things we've learned until we die. Don't be set in your ways—try new things and look at things in a new perspective.

Keep your eyes, ears, and mind open. See things in a different light. Remember why we are coaching—not for us, for the kids. It's always for the kids. I hope I have helped, in any form or fashion, in trying to see things through the kids' eyes. Coach with warmth and compassion, be creative and excite the mind, and always make it fun. As I stated earlier, winning will be a byproduct of listening, trying, and having fun in practice. Thanks, and God bless.

References

Bobby Knight
Yogi Berra
Steve Stone
Joe Jake
Shawn Wilson

Review Requested:

If you loved this book, would you please provide a review at Amazon.com?

www.ingramcontent.com/pod-product-compliance
Lightning Source LLC
Chambersburg PA
CBHW051603120626
46551CB00013B/1644